P9-ECL-293

# GALAXY OF SUPERSTARS

Ben Affleck

Backstreet Boys

Garth Brooks

Mariah Carey

Cameron Diaz

Leonardo DiCaprio

Tom Hanks

Hanson

Jennifer Love Hewitt

Lauryn Hill

Ewan McGregor

Mike Myers

'N Sync

LeAnn Rimes

Britney Spears

Spice Girls

Jonathan Taylor Thomas

Venus Williams

## CHELSEA HOUSE PUBLISHERS

GALAXY OF SUPERSTARS

# Lauryn Hill

## Meg Greene

CHELSEA HOUSE PUBLISHERS
Philadelphia

Frontis: *Lauryn Hill holds the Bible as she accepts the Best New Artist award at the 1999 Grammy Awards. Lauryn often mentions her faith in God. When she quoted Scriptures in accepting one Grammy award, she was sincerely thanking God for her success.*

Produced by
21st Century Publishing and Communications, Inc.
New York, New York
http://www.21cpc.com

CHELSEA HOUSE PUBLISHERS

Editor in Chief: Stephen Reginald
Managing Editor: James D. Gallagher
Production Manager: Pamela Loos
Art Director: Sara Davis
Director of Photography: Judy L. Hasday
Senior Production Editor: LeeAnne Gelletly
Publishing Coordinator: James McAvoy
Assistant Editor/Project Editor: Anne Hill
Cover Designer: Terry Mallon

Front Cover Photo: Ilpo Musto/London Features Int'l
Back Cover Photo: Gie Knaeps/London Features Int'l

The Chelsea House World Wide Web address is
http://www.chelseahouse.com

First Printing

1 3 5 7 9 8 6 4 2

Library of Congress Cataloging-in-Publication Data

Greene, Meg.
  Lauryn Hill / Meg Greene.
   64 p.    cm. – (Galaxy of superstars)
  Includes bibliographical references and index.
  Summary: A biography of the young African American singer from New
Jersey who won five Grammy awards in 1999, including Best New Artist.
  ISBN 0-7910-5495-0 (hc). — ISBN 0-7910-5496-9 (pb).
  1. Hill, Lauryn—Juvenile literature  2. Singers—United States—Biography—
Juvenile literature.  [1. Hill, Lauryn.  2. Singers  3. Women—Biography
4. Afro-American—Biography.]   I. Title.  II. Series.
ML3930.H55G74    1999
782.421649'092—dc21
[b]                                                              99—40740
                                                                    CIP
                                                                     AC

# CONTENTS

# 1

# QUEEN OF
# THE HILL

On January 5, 1999, the 41st annual Grammy nominations announced in Los Angeles celebrated the "Year of the Woman." In almost all categories, female artists dominated. Shania Twain, Sheryl Crow, Madonna, Brandy, and Celine Dion were among the more prominent nominees. Especially noteworthy was the category of Album of the Year, in which all the nominees were women! As one music observer remarked, "It's a testament to girl power."

One name, however, overshadowed all others. A 23-year-old rap, hip-hop, and R&B (rhythm-and-blues) artist from South Orange, New Jersey, emerged as the brightest star in the musical heavens. Her name glittered in three different categories: pop, R&B, and rap. In all, 10 nominations went to Lauryn Hill, a relative newcomer to the pop music scene. The list seemed endless and included Best Female Pop Vocal Performance, Best Female R&B Vocal Performance, Best Rap Solo Performance, Best R&B Song, Best Album, and Best New Artist. Formerly a member of the rap group the Fugees, Lauryn was now a solo artist, writer, producer, and mother of two.

Lauryn's first solo effort, *The Miseducation of Lauryn Hill*, clearly was a winner. The album incorporated a diverse

---

*Lauryn performs "To Zion" at the 1999 Grammy Awards. She became the first woman ever to win five Grammys in one night.*

mix of sounds and styles from classic R&B to reggae, hip-hop, pop, and doo-wop. Tackling themes that ranged from family, relationships, identity, and roles and responsibilities in the community, *The Miseducation of Lauryn Hill* was an ambitious undertaking for a first album. Lauryn not only wrote and sang all the songs but also produced the album.

Lauryn's perseverance and talent had paid off at last. The critical response to the album was exhilarating. Critics hailed her work as a masterpiece that expanded the boundaries of hip-hop, while paying tribute to the soul music of the 1970s. The popular response was just as overwhelming. By the time the Grammy nominations were announced, the album had already sold almost four million copies, and sales showed no sign of slowing down. *The Miseducation* was destined to be a classic.

But Lauryn was no stranger to the Grammys. Two years earlier, in 1997, the Fugees, the rap group of which Lauryn was a member, was nominated as Best New Artist. Because the album that won them the nomination was their second, however, the group was disqualified. Now, just two years later, Lauryn herself had received the same honor. Despite the enthusiastic reception her album had received, however, her nomination as Best New Artist generated controversy. Some in the music business questioned it, believing it was inappropriate. Said one critic, "to have a member of that group be eligible [as a solo artist] is debatable."

Michael Greene, the president of the National Academy of Recording Arts and Sciences (NARAS), who oversaw the awards, defended the choice. Making eligibility a little easier, he suggested, meant more and different kinds of artists would be represented. "You can't penalize someone for coming out of a successful group. When all else fails, we need to err on the side of the artist." This time Lauryn Hill's nomination would stand.

Many insiders in the music industry agreed with Greene. Danyel Smith, editor of *Vibe* magazine, had no doubts who the big winner would be. Lauryn Hill would definitely be the "princess of the evening." Smith added, "I don't think she's going to have a bag big enough to take home all the awards she's going to win."

Lauryn's reaction to the nominations and the turmoil surrounding them was a calm and reserve that made her seem older than her years. In one interview she said, "I definitely appreciate [all the Grammy nominations], but to me it was really powerful when I first released the album . . . and I got to see the reactions first-handedly from the people." She continued, "To me it was a big deal when I met people who'd been touched or inspired [by the music]. . . . That really made me feel better and reconfirmed for me that I was doing the right thing."

Lauryn was philosophical about her chances of winning. She admitted that "awards are always wonderful, wonderful," but also acknowledged that "if I don't get anything that night, I'm cool." She even joked that "I'll have a nice little dress on, get to hang out with my man [Rohan Marley] and look sharp for the evening."

Lauryn needn't have worried. From start to finish, the evening of February 24th was hers. She walked away with five Grammys: Best R&B Song and Female R&B Vocal Performance for "Doo Wop (That Thing)," and Best R&B Album and Album of the Year for *The Miseducation of Lauryn Hill*, marking the first time a hip-hop

*Lauryn's five Grammy awards were only the beginning for her in 1999. She also collected a number of other honors, including three Soul Train Awards, two Billboard Music awards, three NAACP Image Awards, and an American Music Award.*

album has won the award. Despite the controversy, she also won the Grammy for Best New Artist. Her accomplishments on that one evening established a new record for the most awards won by any female artist in the history of the Grammys.

In accepting one award, Lauryn recited from the 40th Psalm: "I waited patiently for the Lord. . . . And he heard my cry. . . . He brought me out of a horrible pit . . . and set my feet upon a rock. . . . He has put a new song in my mouth." Those who knew her understood that

Lauryn did not quote from Scripture simply to create some media hype. Instead she was offering sincere thanks to God for her spectacular success.

After the ceremony, Lauryn was excited but still downplayed her awards. "I feel crazy. . . . I'm kind of in a zone right now," she admitted. But she went on, "I feel very blessed. Who could ask for [this]? An album that I poured my heart and soul into, [and then] to see people receive it like this is a huge reward. I'm very thankful." In discussing her awards, Lauryn also demonstrated her characteristic modesty and poise. "You feel honored that people enjoy—well, not just enjoy or acknowledge—but appreciate what you do," she said. "It's definitely an honor."

For those who supposed that Lauryn Hill was a one-hit wonder, the evening was a revelation. The young woman from South Orange had not only shown she was a serious artist but also achieved her success on her own terms. There could be little doubt in anyone's mind who was the "queen of the hill." Lauryn Hill had come a long way from the days when she sang along to her mother's soul records in the house on Eder Terrace.

# 2

# MUSIC IN
# HER VEINS

Was it just coincidence that Lauryn Hill grew up near Superstar Road? Or were there forces already at work deciding which road she would take?

Born on May 26, 1975, Lauryn was the second child of Mal Hill, a computer consultant, and his wife, Valerie, a high school English teacher. Her parents made their home on Eder Terrace, in one of suburban South Orange, New Jersey's many quiet neighborhoods. Along with her older brother, Malaney, Lauryn and her parents resided in a sturdy red and yellow, two-story brick house with a well-tended yard and garden on a street filled with similar single-family dwellings. All in all it was a picturesque life.

"I wasn't raised rich, " Lauryn stressed. "But I never really wanted the things that we didn't have. I think my parents instilled in us that we didn't need lavish things. As long as we had love and protection, we were always taken care of." There was no shortage of love or encouragement in the Hill household. As a result, Lauryn and her brother flourished.

But gazing out from the second-story attic window, Lauryn saw another world—a world full of concrete, crime,

---

*Lauryn with her mother, Valerie. Lauryn credits her family with providing the love and encouragement she needs to be successful in whatever she attempts.*

and despair. Only a few blocks from the Hills' quiet suburban neighborhood loomed one of South Orange's tougher public housing projects. "I remember looking out this window and there was a certain time of day when the sun used to shine on those buildings and they used to look like gold," Lauryn recalled. "Beautiful. And I'd bug, 'cause I knew they were full of wild people, kids stickin' up each other."

Despite the problems Lauryn saw, however, she characteristically found something positive in the ugliness of the ghetto. "When something is at its worst, there's always something beautiful there too."

Instead of being frightened away from the projects, Lauryn made a point of exploring them. Often she would ride her bicycle to the tough neighborhood and play with the kids who lived there. She even earned a reputation of sorts. "I got my reputation 'cause I could flip. I was a huge tomboy, and I used to do back flips over there in the projects." Unlike the other children who lived there, though, Lauryn could return to a very different world at the end of the day.

Lauryn's parents always encouraged her and her brother in everything they did. They pushed her hard in her studies, even though Lauryn already showed signs of being an overachiever, scoring near-perfect marks in school. After Lauryn finished high school, her parents expected her to go on to college. "When I was a very little girl I wanted to be a superstar/lawyer/doctor. I had an agenda," she said. With her family's encouragement, Lauryn knew there was nothing she couldn't accomplish.

But life in the Hill household was not all work and no play. Lauryn described her father as "the type of [man] who at a wedding would try to breakdance and embarrass us." Both parents joked with their children and were open and friendly. They warmly welcomed their children's friends whenever they stopped by. Lauryn had only the highest words of praise for them. "They were very, very cool."

Lauryn's parents also loved music very much and passed that love on to their children. Mal often moonlighted in the evenings as a singer, working weddings and small clubs around town. Valerie had once studied piano. Malaney played guitar, saxophone, and drums. But as Valerie Hill declared, it was Lauryn who was born with the true musical talent in the family. "Her violin teacher kept telling us, 'I don't believe how musical she is,'" Valerie remembered. Lauryn "just had this effect on people who listened to her."

The Hills made sure their children were exposed to a wide variety of musical styles—everything from show tunes to jazz to pop. But by far the music of choice in the Hill household was the soul music classics of the 1960s and '70s. This was the music of Lauryn's parents' generation—the music they had grown up with, danced to, and fell in love with. In fact long before Valerie even met Mal, she spent her allowance on '45s—small, vinyl discs on which the popular singles of the day had been recorded. These records were called '45s because they spun around the turntable on old phonographs at 45 revolutions per minute (rpms). "I amassed a nice little pile—stacks and stacks of Motown, Philly International, Stax, Marvin [Gaye], Stevie [Wonder], Aretha [Franklin], Donny Hathaway, Gladys Knight—that whole thing," Valerie said. After Lauryn was born, though, Valerie boxed up her beloved records and stored them in the family basement, where they stayed until her

*Lauryn with Babyface (left) and Stevie Wonder (center). As a child, Lauryn loved to play her mother's old Motown and soul music records. Artists such as Stevie Wonder were a strong influence on Lauryn's musical style.*

daughter discovered them.

Whether it was her father practicing his act, songs playing on the stereo or radio, or the popular program *Soul Train* airing on television, Lauryn was surrounded by music. It was, therefore, only a matter of time before, on one of her ventures into the basement, she found her mother's record collection. For Lauryn, it was like an awakening.

"There was something sacred about those old records," Lauryn reminisced. "They meant so much to me, and they kind of had a lot to do with the soundtrack of my life." Her mother agreed. "At the time I didn't know it would have such an impact on Lauryn. But I always felt that she would somehow, some way be involved in music."

Gradually, Lauryn not only uncovered an important part of her mother's past but also learned something about herself. Instead of just listening to the popular songs on the radio or singing the songs she'd known since childhood, Lauryn was learning about music of another kind—soul music. Those records, Lauryn explained, became her "music theory classroom." They also helped her find her talent.

Although Lauryn's parents knew that she had been blessed with a musical aptitude, it wasn't until they heard her singing to their soul records that they realized she had a real gift. Singing soul music seemed to bring out something special in Lauryn's voice and personality. Her mother remembered checking on her at night. Lauryn would be fast asleep with her headphones on, listening to her mother's music. "The '60s soul that I'd collected just seeped into her veins."

By the time she was eight years old, Lauryn had already become the family expert on soul music. At family barbecues she listened to the "oldies" station with the adults. "They'd go, 'Oh, that's Blue Magic!' And I'd go, 'No, it's the Chi-Lites.'" Lauryn was usually right.

It wasn't long before Lauryn began to dream about being a singer. Her mother had made a point of taking her daughter to see plays, musicals, and any type of theater production that they could afford to attend. One experience in particular made an impact on the little girl.

"When she was a girl, I took her to see *Annie*," a popular Broadway musical at the time. "Afterward, Lauryn asked if there could ever be a black Annie."

Lauryn first tested her talent at home, singing for her family and friends. Even when she was a little girl she would entertain her parents in a number of ways. "I would come home from teaching," her mother recalled, "and she'd sit on the floor by my bed while I was taking a nap, and . . . create her own play with her dolls and toys. . . . She could do that for maybe an hour. She would sing to them, she would talk to them; she did lots of things that kept us entertained."

When she was 13, Lauryn took her first step toward realizing her dream of becoming a performing artist. She convinced her father to take her to audition for a spot on *Showtime at the Apollo*, a popular stage production held at the Apollo, a famous theater in Harlem, New York City. The shows at the Apollo featured acclaimed black entertainers and also on occasion showcased young, unknown talent seeking to get a start. Lauryn auditioned and won a chance to perform. Lauryn's mother remembered this momentous occasion: "When the day came, we marshaled the forces, rented a big van, took a bunch of kids from her school for moral support and went off to the Apollo."

Unfortunately, Lauryn's debut got off to a shaky start. Singing Smokey Robinson's "Who's Lovin' You," Lauryn stood so far from the microphone that no one could hear her. Terrified, Lauryn stood there as people started booing. Her uncle, standing in the stage wings, yelled to Lauryn, "Get close to the mike!" Lauryn suddenly grabbed the mike and began singing with a force. Her attitude was "How dare you boo me." In the end, Lauryn triumphed. "She sang her heart out. At the end of the song, they were clapping and screaming for her," her mother recounted.

The experience of performing in public had, nevertheless, taken its toll on Lauryn. After returning home, she began to cry, believing she had let herself down and disappointed her family. Her mother later recalled, "I looked at Lauryn and said, 'Lauryn, they're gonna clap for you one day and maybe not the next, but you gotta take it all. This is part of the business you say you want to be in. Now, if every time they don't scream and holler you're gonna cry, then perhaps this isn't for you.' And she looked at me like I had taken leave of my senses. To her, the mere suggestion that this wasn't for her was crazy."

There could be no doubt about Lauryn's talent and desire. The question now was could she make it in the big time?

# "THIS GIRL CAN SING"

It was 1988 and a new kind music was sweeping the inner city. Called hip-hop, the sound was known for its vigorous beat. The songs were punctuated by rhythmic, rapid vocals sung in "rap" (rhyming) style or "freestyle." The music was often angry, political, and filled with social commentary about black urban life. These were songs almost any kid in the inner city could relate to; hip-hop told the stories of *their* lives and *their* struggles. So it came as no surprise that many black kids dreamed of becoming a master rapper.

At this time, 13-year-old Lauryn Hill was a student at South Orange Middle School. She continued to make excellent grades, became a cheerleader, and was elected president of her class the three years she attended. But what people remember most about Lauryn was that she was as "humble and loving as can be." Johanna Wright, who coached Lauryn in basketball, recalled Lauryn's compassion and budding social consciousness. "She started a breakfast club for the kids who came to school without any breakfast. She would stop on her way to school every day and pick up two or three dozen bagels and some juice."

---

*During her school years, Lauryn carefully balanced her studies and extracurricular activities, as well as the development of her singing career.*

It was around this time that Lauryn met the first of two people who would have a serious impact on her life. Prakazrel Michel, or Pras as he was called, was the son of Haitian refugees whose family had left Haiti in search of a better life in the United States. They had first settled in Brooklyn, where Pras was born. Despite a stable family life and a high IQ, Pras seemed destined to lead the "gangsta" life typical of so many young men in his neighborhood. It took a "gun in my mouth while someone threatened to pull the trigger" to make Pras rethink his options.

By this time, his parents decided the family would be better off in New Jersey. They enrolled Pras at Columbia High School, which was noted for its rigorous academic program. Lauryn's brother Malaney was also a student there. Pras quickly adapted to his new environment, getting good grades and staying away from the gangs. He also had his music. Pras loved hiphop. Early on he had shown a flair for the sound; he was fast, quick-thinking, and could rhyme with the best rappers in the neighborhood. He dreamed of forming his own group and landing a record deal.

But Pras knew he needed a "hook," something different that would get the record companies to notice him and the audience to listen. He thought a group composed of two female singers and a single male rapper would be different enough to get people's attention. He knew one girl, Marcy, who also happened to be a friend of Malaney's. Pras and Marcy approached another girl about singing with the group. "I didn't like the second girl's attitude," Pras recalled in an interview, "and so we cut her loose."

Then Marcy remembered that Malaney's little

*Prakazrel (Pras) Michel, a Haitian immigrant, founded the hip-hop group Tranzlator Crew. The group's name came from the fact that its members rapped in different languages.*

sister Lauryn could sing, really sing. She told Pras, "I know this other girl, but she's real young." (At the time, Lauryn was only 13.) Pras was not persuaded. But Marcy insisted, "This girl can sing. She's baaad." Pras at last relented, inviting Lauryn to come down the House of Music, a small recording studio in West Orange.

The initial meeting went well. Lauryn was impressed with Pras's professional attitude. Pras was equally impressed with Lauryn's voice. Together the three started to practice. Soon they were sounding like a polished group, calling themselves Time. For the first time, Lauryn was getting a sense of what it meant to sing professionally. Her dreams of being a performer were slowly becoming a reality.

Lauryn's confidence in her abilities grew. While still in middle school she was invited to sing the national anthem at a Columbia High School basketball game. LuElle Walker-Peniston, a guidance counselor at Columbia, said in an interview that Lauryn's rendition drove the crowd wild. The counselor added, "She was inspiring. Fans liked her rendition so much that recordings of it were played at subsequent games."

Lauryn recalls this period in her life with happiness. "When I was this kid, I was this sort of bright and shining kid who had a real pure heart and pure spirit. I was real crazy. Everything I did was dramatic. I was wild."

So great was Lauryn's belief in herself that at times she put herself at risk. A family friend recalled the time that Lauryn told everyone she could swim. "A bunch of us went swimming and Lauryn swore up and down that she could swim. I mean, she was trying to tell us how to swim. So we were like 'Okay, let's see how you dive.' We threw her in and she almost drowned. Literally almost drowned."

But that overconfidence didn't mean Lauryn caused trouble. Every Sunday she attended church services with her family. There her voice could be heard singing along with the rest of the congregation. Even at a young age, Lauryn had developed a close relationship with God, from which she would continually draw strength and courage in the years to come.

By 1990 Lauryn had entered Columbia High School. Her excellent grades landed her in the honors program. Her personality won her many friends and admirers. Judy Levy, communications coordinator at the school, remembered Lauryn well. "She was a very good student and the main thing was that she was involved in a lot of things, which is what made her a good student. Whatever she did, she just fit right in." LuElle Walker-Peniston also recognized Lauryn's special qualities. "Lauryn was an excellent student who took advantage of opportunities," she remembered.

In the meantime Lauryn continued to sing her heart out with the group, newly renamed Tranzlator Crew, a reference to the group's particular style of music in which they rapped in different languages. By this time, Pras's cousin, Wyclef Jean, had taken to stopping by when he wasn't working with his own hip-hop group, Exact Change.

Wyclef, or Clef as he was known, was also a Haitian refugee who lived with his family in Brooklyn. His mother's gift of a secondhand guitar had saved him from a life on the streets. After finishing high school, Clef decided he wanted to become a rock star, much to his parent's dismay.

Whenever he met with his cousin Pras, all Wyclef Jean would hear about was how great the two girl singers in Pras's group were. Finally Clef decided he had to hear them for himself and so headed to the House of Music. He had to admit he was impressed by the group, especially Lauryn. When Pras suggested that he do a freestyle rap over one of their songs, he agreed.

The result was magic. Wyclef Jean's vocals

*Wyclef (Clef) Jean joined Tranzlator Crew at the request of his cousin, Pras Michel. The group later changed its name to the Fugees to honor their roots.*

were haunting and intense. He definitely added to the group's overall sound. With encouragement from Marcy and Lauryn, Pras asked Wyclef Jean if he would consider joining Tranzlator Crew. Clef wasn't sure, but he agreed to sit in with the group when he wasn't singing with Exact Change.

By this time the group was spending long hours in the studio practicing and polishing their sound. Pras handled the equipment, with Clef playing occasionally on guitar and sharing the mike with Lauryn. Lauryn, in a later interview, recalled the rigorous schedule she had: "We used to be in the studio from the time after school or track practice until three in the morning. Then I'd go home, go to sleep, wake up at seven and go to school again." But Lauryn loved the routine.

Then, during the next few months, a series of unexpected changes took place. Marcy decided she wanted to go on to college and left the group. Pras also graduated and decided to attend Rutgers, but was not ready to give up on the music yet. Meanwhile Clef parted ways with Exact Change. He had decided to take a chance with Lauryn, Pras, and Tranzlator Crew. Lauryn, too, was performing a careful balancing act between school, her extracurricular activities, and her promising singing career. Nevertheless, the pieces were now in place at last. Tranzlator Crew was about to hit the big time.

# 4

# BLUNTED ON REALITY

To say that Lauryn's life was busy by the time she got to high school is an understatement. She continued to excel at everything she did. A straight-A student, Lauryn loved to read and write poetry. She was the founder of the school's gospel choir, head cheerleader, and a member of the Martin Luther King Jr. Association.

Despite studying hard and being involved in so many activities, Lauryn still found time to socialize, though she avoided any serious romantic entanglements. Her parents learned just how popular she was when Lauryn asked to have a party for her 15th birthday. Lauryn's father agreed that she could have the party in their back yard, on the condition that she invite only her closest friends. Imagine her parent's surprise when 250 people arrived to wish Lauryn a happy birthday.

When she wasn't busy with studying or other school activities, Lauryn hurried to the House of Music to practice with Pras and Clef. Still, Lauryn wasn't about to pin all her hopes on Tranzlator Crew. She had been involved with theater productions at school. She had been told she was good. She wondered how well she would do with acting.

---

*Lauryn has always been interested in performing as well as singing. At 15 she appeared in an off-Broadway hip-hop musical and landed a small role in a soap opera.*

There was only one way to find out.

One day Lauryn informed her parents that she wanted to act and begin going out on auditions. Her parents agreed on one condition. "We made a deal," recalled Valerie Hill. "I said that, as long as her schoolwork came first, I would be happy to chauffeur her to auditions and showcases." True to her word, Lauryn did as she had agreed.

One of her first professional efforts came in 1990 at the age of 15 in an off-Broadway play titled *Club 12*, a hip-hop musical based on William Shakespeare's play *Twelfth Night*. Although the play was not a success, Lauryn's performance drew rave reviews. A theatrical agent noticed her, and not long afterward Lauryn landed a small role in the popular soap opera *As The World Turns*. For the next year, Lauryn worked 12-hour days at the television studio. In her off time, she continued her studies with an on-set tutor.

Lauryn's character, Kirsta Johnson, was the complete opposite of Lauryn. Kirsta was a troubled runaway who was abused and illiterate. Kenyon "Tre" Noble, also a Columbia High School cheerleader, remembers how the other girls would tease Lauryn about her character. "We would shout her lines back to her when she was doing her cheerleading drills. One was 'Don't tell my secret: That I can't read or write.' It made [Lauryn] laugh."

Lauryn's hard work on the soap paid off. The producers, thrilled with her, wanted to renew her contract for another year. But Mal and Valerie Hill believed that Lauryn's education should come first and said no. Lauryn apparently felt the same way and agreed. Besides, her singing career was about to take off.

By 1991 Tranzlator Crew was ready to go public. The group had tacked on "Fugees" (short for refugees) to their name. "Fugees" was a way for Pras and Clef to honor their Haitian roots. By this time Pras was a junior at Rutgers, but he decided to leave school to devote all his time and energy to the group.

The three began working on new material and were excited with the sound they were creating. The group was beginning to combine Haitian rhythms, Jamaican dance hall music, and reggae (another form of Jamaican music) to an overall mix of hip-hop. Pras, Clef, and Lauryn could all handle themselves at the microphone—all were strong singers and rappers. Lauryn especially was beginning to emerge as a powerful and moving vocalist. In time the three became extremely close and saw themselves as members of a family, always looking out for one another.

Lauryn was also beginning to better understand the hip-hop style. She liked the freedom and the spontaneity of the music. She was especially taken with the versatility of hip-hop music. It was always changing, raw and intense one minute, light and even funny the next. Although Lauryn later claimed she had always liked hip-hop, others disagreed. David Sonenberg, who later became the group's manager, remembered that "Lauryn was indoctrinated into hip-hop culture by Clef."

Tranzlator Crew wanted to send a different message from that of other hip-hop groups. So much of the current music dealt with negative themes: violence, drugs, and derogatory images of women. Pras, Clef, and Lauryn instead wanted to celebrate life and to sing about love, respect, and being your own person.

*Carrying a positive message, Lauryn sings, with Pras and Clef in the background. In its early days, Tranzlator Crew performed anywhere they could to increase their visibility—clubs, neighborhood showcases, and even school dances.*

Slowly the group ventured out, playing small clubs, school dances, neighborhood showcases, anywhere they could been seen and heard. Money was not an issue; there was barely enough to pay for gas, but Lauryn loved it all—the grueling schedule, doing her homework in club bathrooms while waiting to perform, getting by on little sleep. The group also shunned doing drugs. Staying focused on the music and the message were what they were about.

"We sang, we rapped, we danced," Lauryn recalled. "As a matter of fact, we were a circus troupe. Maybe we were a little overdeveloped in the sense that we did so much that we were just like, 'Yo, okay, I can do anything.' We were a piece of work but you could see the talent."

The more the group performed, the more its dynamic began to change. Lauryn increasingly commanded center stage. With her good looks, strong voice, and powerful presence, Clef and Pras often found themselves in the background. Pras knew that if it weren't for Lauryn they might not be attracting the attention they were beginning to receive.

Lauryn, though, had mixed feelings about being the primary focus. "There's a lot of shared energy here," she once said. "It was very important for my brothers to shine and, for a period of time, I was almost afraid to shine." Yet, she admitted that a part of her craved the attention and the limelight.

The group's reputation continued to grow. Finally in 1991, Tranzlator Crew found themselves a manager, David Sonenberg. Sonenberg immediately recognized the group's talent and set out to land them a record deal as quickly as possible. He had the group make a demo tape and sent it out to all the major record labels.

Representatives of several record companies asked Tranzlator Crew to audition for them. The auditions proved a disaster. Sonenberg remembers the reactions. "I think it was all too much. These record company guys thought it was some weird stunt. You could see them thinking 'Is it R&B or is it rap?' They should have been thinking it was both."

Everybody declined to invite Tranzlator Crew to record for their company—everybody except the representatives of a small label called Ruff-house Records. The label was considered an upstart and was known for taking chances on groups that no one else would touch. The representatives of Ruffhouse Records liked what they saw and heard and signed Tranzlator Crew to a recording contract.

During the summer of 1991, Tranzlator Crew began work on their first album. It was a painful process as Lauryn, Pras, and Clef labored to make sure everything came out sounding perfect. Gradually they all found their respective niches: Pras handled the technical side of the music, while Clef and Lauryn concentrated on writing the songs. They decided to call the album *Blunted on Reality*, which to them meant being positive on life and about life's choices. By that fall, as Lauryn entered her junior year in high school, the album was finished. Due to internal problems at Ruffhouse Records, however, it would be almost two years before the album was released.

In the meantime the group underwent one last name change. Dropping Tranzlator Crew, the trio now became known simply as the Fugees. "Refugees was always a negative thing. We wanted to make something positive of it," said Wyclef Jean. Lauryn remembered the name change more thoughtfully. "We call ourselves Fugees because we seek refuge in our music. Everybody is seeking refuge from something . . . their jobs, the ghetto, whatever."

With the album done and her character written off *As The World Turns*, Lauryn had a short time to catch her breath and live the life of a normal teenager. She prepared to take her college entrance exams and started seriously to think about going away to college.

It was during this period that Lauryn was offered her first film role, in Steven Soderbergh's 1993 film *King of the Hill.* Lauryn's role was nothing more than a bit part, but she found the experience exciting enough to want to do more. She didn't have long to wait for the opportunity.

Lauryn appeared in film again the following year with *Sister Act 2: Back in the Habit,* starring comedian Whoopi Goldberg. Lauryn's character played a high school "diva with a 'tude." Director Bill Duke remembered how Lauryn made suggestions to improve her character. Recognizing Lauryn's intelligence and talent, Duke let her improvise, especially in a scene where Lauryn's character entertains a class with an impromptu rap. "None of that was scripted," Duke said. "That was all Lauryn. She was amazing."

As soon as she finished making *Sister Act 2,* Lauryn came back to South Orange. The time to decide where to attend college was drawing near. Lauryn received offers from every school to which she had applied: Spelman College, Yale, Columbia, Rutgers, and the University of Pennsylvania. She chose Columbia University, located in New York City. This way she would be close to her family and friends, and still be able to perform and record with the Fugees.

As Lauryn prepared to begin her freshman year at Columbia, the Fugees finally heard the news they had been waiting for: their first album, *Blunted on Reality,* had at last been released.

# 5

# "WE WANTED TO MAKE MUSIC"

*B*lunted on Reality received a mixed popular response. It struggled to number 62 on the *Billboard* magazine Hot 100 chart. (*Billboard* is aimed at the music industry and ranks the popularity of new music releases based on sales.) Although the album wasn't an overwhelming success, people were listening. Selling 130,000 copies, the album at least showed the Fugees had potential.

Critical reaction to the work was even more mixed. Many critics found the unusual fusion of reggae, hip-hop, and Haitian rhythms interesting and appealing. Others, though, wrote the Fugees off as derivative of bigger name groups such as Public Enemy. With European audiences, however, *Blunted on Reality* enjoyed greater popularity and success than it had in the states. Characterizations of the group as "talented songwriters and gifted rappers" and of their music as "brash, smart raps," gave Pras, Clef, and Lauryn reason to feel encouraged about their first effort.

Critics especially singled out Lauryn. They liked what they heard: an angry young woman with a tough style and an amazing voice. *The Source* described Lauryn as "possess[ing] much of the trio's lyrical muscle. She steals

---

*The Fugees perform during a 1997 benefit concert in Haiti. Since Clef and Pras are children of immigrants from Haiti, the group is concerned with the fate of Haitian refugees.*

the show again and again on every track she appears on."

But the group had also learned a valuable lesson. Believing that their sound had been compromised by the demands of Ruffhouse Records, the Fugees vowed next time to record their music *their way*. Lauryn saw it as being true to herself. The Fugees were simply part of a new wave of performers who were not going to create a false image of who and what they were. As she put it, "It's become popular to be stupid, to be violent, to be unintelligent, and that's bad. When people stop being who they are naturally and start pretending to be something negative or not real, that's what's wack."

In the meantime, Lauryn continued with her first year of studies at Columbia. A history major, Lauryn was also taking courses in Spanish as well as serving as tri-captain of the Columbia University cheerleading squad. In the midst of her freshman year, the Fugees decided to hit the road on a tour to promote the *Blunted on Reality* album.

Their live shows went over much better than their efforts in the recording studio. Playing a string of underground clubs and cheap dives, the Fugees started to gain a following composed of both black and white listeners. While Clef and Pras watched over Lauryn, the skinny little girl from South Orange had the crowd eating out of her hand. "She was pretty and she could rhyme. When she opened her mouth and rocked, whoo, child, she had the audience wide open. She was the secret weapon," remembered Harry D'Janite, a former DJ.

Now the group ached to get back to the studio and make another record, hoping to improve on their first endeavor. This time the executives at Ruffhouse Records were convinced the group did have a future and assured them they could make the kind of record they wanted to without interference. That was all the Fugees needed to hear. In 1995, renting a studio in East Orange, New Jersey, called the Booga Basement, the trio went to work. "The production on our last album was wack," Clef said in an interview. "But with the next album, we're not working with the same people. Our next album is going to be the bomb."

Once in the studio, the group began to experience real creative differences during their sessions for the first time. What had once been a friendly competition between Lauryn and Clef over who had the best lyric or rhyme for a song was beginning to turn into angry and emotional arguments. Lauryn was also becoming more aggressive in her demands that a particular song be done her way. While she publicly declared "I was quite content to sing the Fugees' songs," privately it was another matter.

Despite the tensions arising among them, the Fugees managed to record the tracks they needed to make a second album. The result was *The Score*, released in 1996. Driven by Lauryn's rich vocals, the album also showcased the three distinct personalities that composed the Fugees in a way their first effort had not. With its winning combination of soul, reggae, and hip-hop lyrics and rhythms, the album convinced many listeners that the Fugees were no flash-in-the-pan group. Their audience grew.

The group also saw one of their singles, a remake of Roberta Flack's "Killing Me Softly with His Song," become a breakthrough hit. As one writer observed, the Fugees' rendition was "an amazing odyssey" with Lauryn's "alternately soulful and seductive singing."

The response to *The Score* was unbelievable, even to the Fugees themselves. People were buying *The Score* just to listen to that song. It was the breakout hit of the summer. Radio stations around the country played it constantly, while the video became an instant hit on MTV. The song also experienced a similar response in England. Pras was pleased but realistic about the clamor and excitement. "It's great, but it doesn't stop here for us. It's like 'That's cool. You're hot now.' But we've still got work to do, know what I'm saying?"

*The Score* was popular for another reason. Critics saw the album as the first effort to bring older listeners into the hip-hop fold. The album, with its socially conscious themes, also introduced a vision of black empowerment that had rarely been heard in hip-hop before. Lauryn's efforts, as with her other ventures, were directed toward making the music the best it could be. "We wanted to make music for the kids that grew up like us, " she told *Rolling Stone*. "Some people might think 'Well they play instruments so we can make this group more accessible to white folks.' All we're trying to do is bring back a musicality, a raw essence that's been lost."

Yet the time had come for Lauryn to make a painful decision. With the release of the second album and the success of "Killing Me Softly," the group decided to tour the United States and Europe. An extended tour meant missing school, something about which Lauryn, now a sophomore at Columbia, had conflicting emotions. Finally she decided that rather than dropping out, she would request a leave of absence from the school. Her parents supported her decision, agreeing that she needed to find out what her heart wanted her to do. Officials at Columbia also agreed and gave Lauryn a leave of absence for one year.

With school temporarily taken care of, the group set out on a very hectic tour that saw them traveling through most of 1996. Not only did the Fugees play to enthusiastic crowds in the United States and Europe, but they also planned a benefit concert in Haiti in the spring of 1997.

The strain of touring, however, was taking its toll on Lauryn. "We stayed on tour for a long time," she recalled. "Tour[ing] is interesting because it ain't home, which means it's not reality. It's the road. Every night you play for an audience that's clapping for what you do, so you have this warped sense of self."

It was also during this period that Lauryn came closest to admitting to a love relationship with Wyclef Jean. Rumors had circulated almost from the first time they had met, but neither one ever acknowledged the affair. Whatever the truth about her relationship, Lauryn was suffering from a crisis of faith in God. "I stopped praying. And the reason why I stopped praying was because there were some things in my life that I knew weren't good for me. But I had decided to need those things. . . . I knew that if I prayed, God would take them from me. So I was afraid."

Lauryn continued to struggle with her personal life. Her professional life, though, couldn't have been better. Then one night after a concert, Lauryn's life changed forever. Greeting the usual throng of DJs, record reps, and fans, Lauryn noticed a good-looking young man making his way toward her.

That young man had an interesting history of

*Lauryn with boyfriend Rohan Marley. For a long time the couple met in secret in order to avoid media attention.*

his own. Rohan Marley was the son of the late reggae legend, Bob Marley. He was also a well-known college football player who had gone on to star for the Ottawa Roughriders in the Canadian Football League. He began to make small talk with Lauryn. Lauryn's response was guarded.

But Rohan didn't give up. At the infrequent breaks in the Fugees' tour, Rohan and Lauryn began dating. Soon the couple fell in love. They continued meeting in secret, however, not wanting their relationship to come to the attention of

the media. "He came to me when I wasn't looking for anybody. I'd never met anyone like him."

Despite the upheaval in her private life,
Lauryn still made time to help out others. One
of her first undertakings was founding the
Refugee Project, an outreach organization to
raise money for orphans and Haitian refugees
in the United States. At the same time she
started a day camp for inner-city children that
would keep them off the streets and out of
trouble. Another project, "Hoodshock," which
staged a series of free concerts to boost voter
registration among young adults, was not as
successful. A stampede broke out at the first
concert, and 30 spectators were injured.

All things considered, though, 1996 was an
exceptional year for Lauryn and the Fugees.
During 1996 the Fugees changed from being
just one among many hip-hop bands to one of
the most popular groups in the world. They
had won an MTV Video Music Award for
"Killing Me Softly with His Song," and there
was talk that they would earn some Grammy
nominations as well.

But by Christmas, Lauryn found herself physi-
cally exhausted and complained of having diffi-
culty concentrating. She went to the doctor for a
checkup and got a piece of unexpected news
that made 1996 an even more remarkable year
for her. The 21-year-old singer was pregnant.

# 6

# "I Am Not
a Racist"

By the end of 1996, Lauryn Hill found herself at a cross-roads personally and professionally. She had emerged as one of hip-hop's newest stars. Because of her honesty, beauty, intelligence, and talent, she had become a role model for young women the world over. But now she was unmarried and pregnant. What was she going to do?

As soon as her condition became public knowledge, many wondered who the father of the child was. Trying desperately to keep Rohan's identity and their relation-ship a secret, Lauryn refused to name the father.

She also faced an even more serious problem. Should she keep the baby? She remembered people telling her, "Girl, you've got a career. Don't be having no baby now." Others criticized Lauryn for setting a poor example for young girls, especially young black girls, by having a child out of wedlock. Music business associates and personal friends warned her that her career could stall if she had a baby. Lauryn was truly caught in a dilemma.

Describing the episode later, Lauryn revealed that she had to look deep within herself for an answer. "I looked at myself in the mirror and I said, 'Okay, now this is the hard

*A pregnant Lauryn pauses during a video shoot. As her pregnancy progressed, Lauryn faced increased—and unwanted—media interest.*

one,' and I prayed on it. What I do know is that God is never going to give you a sign to not have a child if you are pregnant. . . . In my brain I said, 'I'm okay financially. I have a man in my life who loves me. I have a supportive family. I believe I would be a good mother.' I said, 'Wow, the only reason for me not to have this child is because it would inconvenience me.'"

As Lauryn had hoped, Rohan and her parents supported her decision. Her bandmates, while pleased for Lauryn, were worried about the Fugees' other commitments. Lauryn, however, reassured them that she would continue to work with the group as long as she could.

The extent of those prior commitments kept Lauryn going for almost seven months. She went on tour, performing in baggy clothes to hide her pregnancy. But once off stage, she retired to her room to catch up on her sleep and satisfy what had become a craving for gritty foods such as cornstarch and even baking soda!

As rumors about her pregnancy spread, Lauryn found herself facing more and more unwanted media attention about her condition and the identity of the father. As hard as she tried, it became increasingly difficult for Lauryn to remain polite and composed when barraged with questions about her private life that she felt were nobody's business. The pressure, combined with her morning sickness and general fatigue, caught up with Lauryn in early 1997. When an interviewer continued pressing Lauryn about her pregnancy, she replied "I know this is your job, but this is my life." The interviewer backed off.

Despite the growing turmoil in her personal life, the Fugees' popularity continued to grow. In January 1997 the group received two Grammy

nominations, one for Best Rap Album for *The Score* and the other for Best R&B Performance by a Duo or Group for their hit single, "Killing Me Softly with His Song." The group was invited to perform at the Grammy Awards show in February. They appeared on stage three times that evening: once for performing, and the other two times to receive their Grammys. They had won in each category. The awards were not only a sign that hip-hop had entered the mainstream music world but also an acknowledgment that

*The Fugees perform at the 1996 MTV Video Music Awards. The group was also invited to perform at the 1997 Grammys and received two awards there.*

Lauryn, Pras, and Clef had paid their dues and made it to the top. Now they would have to find a way to stay there.

The evening, though, ended on something of a sour note for Lauryn. She was pleased with the Fugees' awards and the success of their CD. (*The Score* had sold 14 million copies.) But she was troubled that the majority of the album's buyers seemed to be middle-class whites. It was ironic, she felt, that an African-American group such as the Fugees, who wrote and sang about social and political issues concerning blacks, were now regarded as hip among whites. The only reason whites were buying their music, Lauryn thought, was because they wanted to appear cool, not because they understood who and what the Fugees were really about.

By the time of the Grammy Awards, Lauryn was ready to speak her mind. Both in her acceptance speech and later at a post-awards interview, Lauryn expressed her views about the music industry and its problems. She also hoped that in the future more blacks and fewer white people would buy the Fugees' albums.

Lauryn had not anticipated the controversy she aroused. Not long afterward, an anonymous caller to radio "shock-jock" Howard Stern said that Lauryn Hill had remarked in an interview that she "would rather see babies starve than have white people buy Fugees' records."

The backlash was as passionate as it was unexpected. Both Pras and Clef defended Lauryn, saying she was no racist and that their music was for all people, not just blacks. Lauryn herself tried to clarify what she had said, telling one interviewer that her remarks had been "twisted" and emphatically stating that "I don't have hate for anybody. I grew up with everybody." She even called a radio station to deny the charge on the air. "I said, 'How can I possibly be a racist? My music is universal music. And I believe in God. If I believe in God, then I have to love all of God's creations. There can be no segregation.'"

Despite the dispute, the Fugees' records continued to sell. Many people realized that whatever Lauryn might have said, she was becoming an established and powerful presence in the music industry. Because of her prominence and appeal, many were reluctant to clash with her.

The unfortunate incident continues to haunt Lauryn to this day. The accusations of racism are often repeated in Internet chat rooms and message boards, leading to critical observations like the one from a teenager who wrote, "I think they should lock her [Lauryn] up just for saying that." In an interview published in *Teen People* in April 1999, Lauryn commented, "From this one broadcast, all of a sudden people who appreciated my music thought there was something wrong with who I was and what I represented. . . . Let me clarify this right now. I am not a racist. If you're a good person with a good heart, you're cool with me. And I hope I'm cool with you."

After the Grammys, the Fugees again went on tour. This time they performed throughout England and Europe. In April 1997 the group played a benefit concert in Haiti that was of great personal significance to them. While in Haiti, President René Preval presented Lauryn, Pras, and Clef with the Medal of Honor for their great efforts.

Then the Fugees returned to the studio to contribute songs for two soundtracks: "Rumble

*Lauryn and the Fugees are awarded the Medal of Honor by Haitian President René Preval (left, with Lauryn). The group, whose name is short for "refugees," staged concerts to benefit Haitian refugees expelled from the Dominican Republic.*

in the Jungle" for *When We Were Kings*, a film about the legendary heavyweight boxer, Muhammad Ali, and "The Sweetest Thing," for the movie *Love Jones*. One of the few projects Lauryn did turn down was the chance to be in the film version of *Beloved*, starring Oprah Winfrey and based on Toni Morrison's novel about the tragic legacy of slavery.

Finally Lauryn realized she needed to slow down a little. She began writing songs on her own. She watched as Pras and Clef continued working in the studio on solo projects. She contributed songs and vocals to each of their efforts. Lauryn even started to think seriously about making an album of her own, something she had actually been contemplating for some time. Little did she realize where these musings would take her.

# 7

# *"EXPECT POSITIVITY"*

While awaiting the birth of her first child, Lauryn continued to ponder striking out on her own. In fact her pregnancy, rather than slowing her down, actually increased her creative energies. "I had so much energy," she recalled in an interview, "I was bouncing off the walls." She elaborated further to another interviewer in 1998: "My mind and ability to create expanded. I had the desire to write in a capacity that I hadn't done in a while. . . . I was very much in touch with my feelings at the time."

Writing at a furious pace, Lauryn completed more than 30 songs by the summer of 1997. Not content only to write and perform, Lauryn also took on the job of producing one of the tracks, "On That Day," a song she wrote for gospel singer CeCe Winans. Then, while at work in a Detroit recording studio, she went into labor during the session. On August 3, 1997, Lauryn Hill and Rohan Marley became the parents of a little boy. They named him Zion. Lauryn still refused, however, to reveal the name of the child's father. Her reason? "I felt like the world had enough of me. I felt like I put my soul on records, and I didn't have to answer any global questions about who my boyfriend was."

---

*Lauryn sings at a 1999 concert in Germany. When asked what her fans could look forward to in her tour, Lauryn said, "Expect positivity."*

Lauryn approached motherhood like she did everything else in her life: with enthusiasm, integrity, and passion. Yet the new responsibilities of having a child did not stop her from pursuing her career. Within a few months of Zion's birth, Lauryn was back in Detroit, this time to produce another track she had written for the "Queen of Soul," Aretha Franklin. Lauryn not only produced "A Rose Is Still a Rose" for Aretha's album but also directed the accompanying video. Lauryn was thrilled to work with one of her childhood idols, declaring "Aretha's so baaad." Aretha was also taken with Lauryn and her talents, calling her "positive, detailed, conscientious. Frankly, I was surprised to see that in such a young woman."

After finishing her producing and directing duties, Lauryn returned to New Jersey with serious intentions—to begin working on her first solo album. She had decided to stay in South Orange to be near her family and friends. She, Rohan, and Zion eventually moved into her childhood home, after Lauryn bought a new home down the street for her parents. "I have everything I need there," she said of her hometown. "That place keeps me very familiar with who I am."

Not long after, she bundled up Zion and headed off to Tuff Gong Studios in New York City to begin recording what would become *The Miseducation of Lauryn Hill.* In trying to explain her vision of the album, Lauryn stated, "I wanted a hip-hop album that has the roots, the integrity, and the sound of an old record. I wanted the kids on the street to hear the hip-hop element and yet be exposed to the musicality, to realize that the two don't have to be mutually exclusive." For Lauryn it was simply a matter of sharing

*The "Queen of Soul,"
Aretha Franklin, at the
1999 Daytime Emmy
Awards. Lauryn wrote
and produced "A Rose
Is Still a Rose" for
Aretha's new album.
She was thrilled to be
able to work with one
of her childhood idols.*

her own musical education with the world.

Staying true to her belief that she creates music for everyone, *The Miseducation of Lauryn Hill* incorporated a number of different musical styles. Using the rhythms and strains of hip-hop, pop, R&B, and doo-wop, it was as if Lauryn were writing a musical history of her fears, her hopes, her passions, her life, herself.

Returning to the recording studio to realize her personal musical vision had a deep impact on Lauryn. The final product of Lauryn's efforts is a deeply intimate album that reflects on everything from loss to love, from the celebration of the birth of her son to criticism of "wannabes" in today's music scene. Several songs were rumored to be about Clef and their relationship, but Lauryn has never admitted that that was the case. What does come through in several of the songs is Lauryn's deep religious faith.

Lauryn not only wrote all the songs for *The Miseducation of Lauryn Hill* but also produced them, stating that the "album was becoming so personal, I knew I had to do it myself." She insisted on having musicians with her in the studio, rather than simply adding vocals to prerecorded or synthesized tracks. "It was my idea to record it so the human element stayed in. I didn't want it to be too technically perfect." Lauryn also drew on the talents of several "guest stars," including hip-hop singer Mary J. Blige, the legendary guitarist Carlos Santana, and crooner D'Angelo. But Lauryn did not invite two friends to join in the studio sessions: Pras and Clef were conspicuously absent.

Although Lauryn may have exercised total control over her project, she admitted in one interview that executives at Ruffhouse Records were less than enthusiastic about the direction the work was taking. "You have to assert yourself. I think when you're a woman you have to assert yourself even a little more. The record companies . . . think when you win with a formula why change the formula? But if you're trying to be an artist, then the idea is to grow and to not stay stagnant." There were also doubts that Lauryn could handle producing an entire album on her own. She eventually silenced her critics as the engineers and musicians who worked with her lauded her abilities as a producer.

In the end, Lauryn believed that her songs and making the album had "purged her soul." "What's in that record, to me, is a movement from a darker space and return to a brighter space." From a little girl singing along to her mother's soul music records, to the political and social awareness of a young woman, to a pop superstar, to a loving mother, Lauryn had given the public a hard and honest look at her soul.

By the time *The Miseducation of Lauryn Hill* was released in August of 1998, Lauryn was seven months pregnant with her second child. In November she gave birth to a baby daughter named Selah Louise. Meanwhile, Lauryn waited anxiously to learn the response to her new album. There was no cause for concern. *The Miseducation of Lauryn Hill* sold more copies during its first week in stores than any album by a female artist had ever sold in a comparable period of time. The record was a smash hit!

Critical response was equally inspiring. Some critics considered Lauryn's debut a masterpiece, and many predicted it would quickly become a hip-hop classic. Others announced that Lauryn had paved the way for a "neo-soul" sound and that *Miseducation* broke new ground with its blending of several musical genres. Lauryn was elated. "I think it is a strong statement . . . that I can make an album completely from my soul and without compromise and be acknowledged for it," she explained.

Another indication of the popularity of the album was the number of awards it received. In addition to her five Grammys, Lauryn collected three Soul Train Awards, two Billboard Music Awards, three NAACP Image Awards, and an American Music Award, as well as numerous other honors from a variety of entertainment publications.

By June 1999, *The Miseducation of Lauryn Hill* had sold well over 40 million copies. It has been designated as a gold, platinum, double platinum, and triple platinum record. "Doo Wop (That Thing)" also did well as a single, selling over one million copies and thus by itself earning the status of a gold record.

What lies ahead for Lauryn Hill? Currently, the 24-year-old mother of two continues to work as hard as ever, while striving to balance her personal and professional lives. She remains dedicated to her organization, the Refugee Project, which has already sent hundreds of inner-city kids to camp and helped register thousands of voters.

In addition to recording and performing, Lauryn also wants to act in more films. At present she is reviewing dozens of scripts. Two possible projects are a film version of the Broadway play *Dreamgirls* and a remake of the classic *A Star Is Born* with actor and singer Will Smith. Lauryn, though, isn't just waiting around for the right project to materialize. She recently formed her own film production company to help her find "something new and original" to do.

As far as her personal life goes, Lauryn and Rohan are still together, although they haven't married. For a brief moment in January 1999, they suffered a near tragedy. Waiting for Lauryn to finish work at the studio, Rohan fell asleep in the car with the motor running. The car caught fire and an electronic malfunction disabled the locks and windows. Rohan was trapped inside the car. Called to the scene, police smashed the windshield and Rohan escaped, shaken but

*Lauryn performs at the 1999 Soul Train Music Awards in Los Angeles. That night she took home awards for Best R&B/Soul/Rap Album of the Year, Best Female R&B/Soul/Rap Single of the Year, and Best Music Video.*

unharmed. Not long after the incident, the couple appeared together in public for the first time.

Lauryn has said they do plan to marry, but when they do, the ceremony will be small and a strictly private affair. "My relationship isn't a publicity stunt. We don't do things to get in the paper. We just live," she has been quoted as saying.

Many fans wonder if they have seen the last of the Fugees. None of the members will say for sure. When pressed, Lauryn admits to uncertainty about the future of the group. She hasn't seen either Pras or Clef in some time, but has also said, "I don't look at it like we're broken up, but we just don't have any plans right now. Right now I want to perform on my own and take this album to the people live."

To that end, Lauryn kept busy planning her 1999 tour. She hit the road with Atlanta-based hip-hoppers OutKast in a 22-date tour of cities throughout the United States. What can her fans expect to see? For starters, Lauryn will be traveling with a band, a rare sight among hip-hop acts. Included will be a horn section, a guitarist, and two D.J.s. And, oh yes, "Expect positivity," says Lauryn. Naturally, "positivity" has by now became one of her trademarks.

In all respects, Lauryn Hill has established herself as a guiding force on today's music scene, as popular with white audiences as with black. At the same time, her work has won critical acclaim. Many young women hold Lauryn in high regard as a role model. She has shown that through determination, persistence, and hard work, dreams can come true. Today, Lauryn is living her fantasy, doing exactly what she has always wanted to do. For Lauryn Hill— mother, singer, composer, producer, actress, and social activist—music has truly become the "soundtrack" of her life.

# CHRONOLOGY

1975   Born Lauryn Hill on May 26 in South Orange, New Jersey, to Mal and Valerie Hill.

1988   Makes her singing debut at *Showtime at the Apollo*; meets Pras Michel and Wyclef Jean and begins working as part of Tranzlator Crew, later to become the Fugees.

1991   Lands a television role in the soap opera *As The World Turns.*

1992   Films *King of the Hill.*

1993   Appears in the film *Sister Act 2: Back in the Habit.*

1994   The Fugees' first album, *Blunted on Reality,* released.

1996   The Fugees' second album, *The Score,* released; meets Rohan Marley.

1997   First child, Zion, is born; begins work on first solo effort.

1998   *The Miseducation of Lauryn Hill* is released; second child, Selah Louise, is born.

1999   Wins five Grammy Awards, the first woman ever to do so; tours U.S.

# ACCOMPLISHMENTS

**Albums (Fugees)**

1994   *Blunted on Reality*

1996   *The Score*
       *Bootleg Versions*

**Singles (Fugees)**

1994   "Boof Baf"
       "Nappy Heads"
       "Vocab"

1996   "Fu-Gee-La"
       "Ready or Not"
       "Killing Me Softly with His Song"

**Soundtrack Contributions (Fugees)**

1997   "Rumble in the Jungle" (from *When We Were Kings*)
       "The Sweetest Thing" (from *Love Jones*)

1998   "Just Happy to Be Me" (from *Elmopalooza!*)

### Albums (Solo)

1998   *The Miseducation of Lauryn Hill*

### Singles (Solo)

1998   "Doo Wop (That Thing)"
       "Ex-Factor"
       "Everything Is Everything"

### Soundtrack Contributions (Solo)

1999   *The Mod Squad*

### Filmography

1992   *King of the Hill*
1993   *Sister Act 2: Back in the Habit*

### Television

1991   *As the World Turns*

# AWARDS

### Fugees

1996   MTV Music Award for R&B Video of the Year

1997   Grammy Awards for Best Rap Album and Best R&B Performance by a Duo or Group

### Lauryn Hill

1998   *Billboard* Music Awards for Best R&B Album and Best R&B/Urban Artist Video Clip; American Music Award for Favorite New Soul/R&B Artist; Essence Award; Grammy Awards for Album of the Year, Best New Artist, Best R&B Song, Best Female R&B Vocal Performance, and Best R&B Album of the Year; NAACP Image Awards for Outstanding New Artist, Outstanding New Female Artist, and Outstanding Album; President's Award; *USA Today* Best R&B Album of the Year

1999   Soul Train Awards for Best R&B/Soul/Rap Album of the Year, Best Female R&B/Soul/Rap Single of the Year, Best Music Video; Sammy Davis Jr. Award for Entertainer of the Year (shared with R. Kelly); World Music Awards for Best R&B Female Artist, Best Rap Female Artist, and Best New Artist; *Details* Artist of the Year; *Entertainment Weekly* Top-10 Entertainers of the Year; *New York Times* for Number-One Album of the Year; *Rolling Stone* for Best Album of the Year, Best Female Artist, and Best R&B Artist; *Spin* for Artist of the Year; *Time* for Number-One Album of the Year; MTV Video Music Awards for Best Female Video, Best R&B Video, and Video of the Year

# FURTHER READING

Nickson, Chris. *Lauryn Hill: She's Got That Thing.* New York: St. Martin's Press, 1999.

Powell, Kevin. "Lauryn Hill: She Knows Why the Caged Bird Sings." *Horizon Magazine*, 1998.

Shapiro, Marc. *My Rules: The Lauryn Hill Story.* New York: Berkley Boulevard Books, 1999.

# ABOUT THE AUTHOR

MEG GREENE earned a bachelor's degree in history at Lindenwood College in St. Charles, Missouri, and masters degrees from the University of Nebraska at Omaha and the University of Vermont. Ms. Greene is the author of two other books, writes regularly for *Cobblestone Magazine* and other publications, and serves as a contributing editor for *Suite101.com's* "History For Children." She makes her home in Virginia.

# INDEX